TIFFANY TELLS TESTIMONIES

SELF-REFLECTION AND SHORT STORIES OF GOD'S DELIVERANCE AND SALVATION

(REFLECTION QUESTIONS INCLUDED)

BY

TIFFANY NAPIER

Tiffany Tells Testimonies
Self-reflections and short stories of God's deliverance and salvation

Copyright © 2024 by Tiffany Napier

Published by Tiffany Napier
Produced by Create and Blossom
712 Austin Avenue
Waco, TX 76701
www.createandblossomstudios.com

ISBN: 978-1-945304-41-5 paperback
ISBN: 978-1-945304-43-9- eBook

Printed in the United States of America

First Edition

TABLE OF CONTENTS

INTRODUCTION

Can I be transparent with you? I'm not a book reader. I only used to read books for assignments and prizes, never really out of enjoyment. It reminds me of elementary school when we'd read thick chapter books and only take a test of 10 questions. The bonus was that the bigger the book, the bigger the points and all the points led to a prize. I won't lie; I would skim through the book as best as possible and take my chance at the test. Most of us only want to obtain information if it is relevant or if we can get something out of it. So often, we wish this was the case for a test that God allows on our journey. We get these grand assignments with the hope of skipping over the part of the pain, sadness, disappointment, and frustration just to get to the good part…the blessing. In this life, there is no skipping, only choices, decisions, and delays, with the hope that our bodies can endure it all before the inevitable expiration date.

Every part of my journey is valid, the good, the good, and the good, with the understanding that all things (painful and traumatic) are truly working out for God's good in me. When I preach, I often disclaim that I will give you what the Lord gave me and then sit down. Understanding what the Lord gives me to share is enough.

This book contains short but weighty testimonies of God's faithfulness in my life. I'm giving you the meat, but I plan to provide the sides in future books. The Lord is really cool. Each chapter is the title of its own book, which will be dispersed in the future.

In this book, I will be sharing traumatic events. Please take care of yourself while reading this book. Take Care= deep breaths, taking breaks, processing with a therapist, journaling, reading with a group for support, etc. Coping mechanisms are the clutch that is used to read traumatic things. My intentions are not to trigger anyone but to tell my raw truth, hoping for relativity and healing. At the end of each chapter is a chance to Reflect on practical ways to implement coping mechanisms and questions for self-reflection or group discussion to help process. This would not be possible without the Holy Spirit's guidance. I'm thankful for the solid courage of the Lord and for being able to share these parts of myself. May these stories bring healing to you as I am healing even now.

CHAPTER 1

HOW REJECTION TRIED TO STEAL MY IDENTITY

"I'm coming out. I want the world to know. Got to let it show" was never one of my anthems while I was in the homosexual lifestyle. I was comfortable keeping my lifestyle a secret to a certain extent. I was comfortable sharing amongst others who were in that lifestyle or when someone would attempt to hit on my girl. I was *uncomfortable* around family, church settings, and people who thought highly of me.

The enemy comes to steal, kill, and destroy. One way he does this is through rejection. If he can contaminate what we believe about ourselves, implant fear of being accepted by others, and make us hate ourselves, then he has successfully stolen our identity.

Identity is tricky these days. I remember hearing that pink means girl and blue means boy. Now, parents give their children the right to choose their gender, name, ethnicity, etc. A name or label speaks volumes of what a child will actually become.

The power of labels can easily construct who we become. If someone is speaking false identities over you, you can become that. For example, if someone calls you a "Tomboy," you gon be just like your sorry daddy, or, "you ghetto," or you wrong." Life and death are in the power of the tongue. You can birth life or death over a child before they are even conceived. But the power of the living word of God being prayed and spoken over a child's identity births life. Since God is ultimately the one who formed us in our mother's womb, wouldn't he have the right to tell us who we will become?

My dad labeled me a tomboy; a "tomboy" is a girl who likes or does boy things. This name held weight to how I was perceived and conducted myself. My dad introduced me to sports at the age of five. Back in my day, the teams were co-ed. I was a natural athlete and was often the star of my teams. Most people complimented me for how good I was. I even heard other parents saying I was better than the boys. So… I was labeled as a tomboy, and hearing I was better than boys began to shape how I saw myself. I rejected everything girl-like. I didn't like pink, purses, make-up, etc. I remember even my mom sending me to school in dresses, and I would bring a change of athletic gear. Changing my clothes worked until my teacher snitched on me; shout out to that teacher...you know who you are. This mindset became the base of my identity. The narrative, I believe, ultimately, is that who you are is not good enough; be someone else.

My identity, aka my soul, was controlled by 3 ruler spirits. Rejection, Rebellion, and Bitterness. Rejection is what I thought(mind/emotion) believed about myself and others, Rebellion is what I acted out in (will), and bitterness is what I felt(emotional).

For me, rejection evoked the most visceral behavior. Notice I say behavior, which is *an organism's activities in response to external or internal stimuli*. A behavior is a response to something or someone that has affected you, either internally (inner)or externally(outward). I struggled with fear of rejection by people or situations and self-rejection. Rejection is refusing to accept, use, or believe someone or something. Being in the homosexual lifestyle in and out for sixteen years consumed literally everything and everyone connected to me. I experienced multiple near-death situations, drugs, sex, alcohol, stealing, cheating, confusion, suicidal thoughts, guilt, and shame. I didn't like myself, but I wanted everyone to think/believe that I did. I always strived to put my best foot forward, hiding behind my accomplishments, abilities, and big personality so others couldn't see the pain I was running from and never wanted to acknowledge.

REFLECTIONS

Ways to regulate yourself…

Let's take some deep breaths! Breath in through your nose, and out through your mouth! Do this as much as needed!

Questions:

What is your personal definition of identity? Who has influenced what you believe about yourself? God? Family? The church? Parental figures? Social media? Coaches? And how have they shaped the way you see yourself?

Rejection, Rebellion and Bitterness are strong words to describe emotions. Have you ever experienced any one of them? If so, in what ways?

In what ways have/can you confront rejection, rebellion or bitterness? (ex. forgive yourself and others, seek mental health counseling, form a support group amongst friends)

CHAPTER 2

70X7

In 2013, I heard the voice of my offender in the nursing home facility which smelled like urine and tissues. I couldn't believe that after seventeen years I still recognized his voice.

Three days earlier, I had sought the Lord in my quiet place and heard him whisper the word forgiveness. My pride was at an all-time high, and I was self-righteous to be exact. What did the Lord have to teach me about forgiveness? I had been walking with the Lord for only two months and felt like I had become all-knowing.

He spoke to me, saying, "I want you to forgive your offender."

I responded, "Of course, Lord, I forgive the man that raped me repeatedly for months at the age of 9; in Jesus' name, Amen". My prayer was quick and straight to the point.

But the Lord responded, "I receive your prayer, but I want you to forgive him in person."

I immediately felt anger rise up in my chest. I told the Lord, "I'll forgive him in person, alright, with these two fists." I wanted revenge with violence. He was three-times bigger than I was at the age of nine, it was not a fair fight. By this time I was twenty-six, physically fit due to workouts from playing college basketball and rugby. A vow I hid in my heart is that when I saw him again he would "get this work, on sight" aka I would beat him up immediately.

The Lord didn't respond, he allowed me to sit with my anger. Then I lamented, "I don't even know where he is or if he is still alive." The Lord responded, "I will guide you; do not fear; I am with you."

That day, I discovered he was alive and located where he was. It was even brought to my attention that he had dementia. I was like, "Lord, you want me to forgive someone who won't even remember me? The Lord spoke and said, "he will remember you; do not fear; I will be with you."

REFLECTIONS

Ways to regulate yourself…

Let's notice what sensations you're feeling in your body. Close your eyes while sitting in an upright position, focus on your breath by taking 3 deep breaths. In through your nose and out through your mouth slowly. If the sensation is still there, focus on the area you feel it and use your breath to release it(example)If you're feeling anxiety in your chest, focus on your chest and take deep breaths to release the feeling until it is gone.

Questions

It's been said that forgiveness is for you and not the other person. Is there someone that has come to mind that you need to forgive?

Has the Lord ever called you to do something and you didn't want to do it? What was your response? Did you do it? If you did it, how did you feel afterward? If you didn't do it, ask the Lord and others to encourage you towards taking the steps to do it.

Anger is an emotion that most people try to deny or hide, mostly due to fear of how it will come out/be expressed or what people will think. How do you deal with Anger? Helpful ways to cope…acknowledge it, try your best to express it in a way that will not be harmful to you or others, move your body…it's important to know anger is not bad and there are healthy ways to express it.

PRACTICAL IMPLICATION TO

RELEASE ANGER

Write down what you may be angry about on a piece paper (sentences are not required, you can simply write words)

Next, take the piece of paper with the words you wrote on it, rip it to pieces or ball it up

Lastly, visualize yourself releasing your anger into a place that is disconnected from you, Find the nearest trashcan and throw the pieces or ball away, take deep breaths as needed to help regulate any sensations.

CHAPTER 3

BEING PRESENT IN PAIN.

In 2014, my parents died at the age of 48, 5 months apart. My dad died in July and my mom in December. It was a traumatic pain. What I realized quickly after their departure, is that I lived for them. They were my idols; I could not fathom the point of life without them. I quickly began to understand the hard truth. Life did not revolve around me and people were going to continue to live even while I lived through death. I had to become present in this undeniable pain.

In my life, I've learned that both pain and present cancel each other out. If I was in pain, being present was few and far between. If I was present then I was suppressing my pain.

Pain is something that is impossible to escape. The hard part about pain is that it can manifest itself in multiple ways. It can be physical, mental, spiritual, and emotional. Pain is one of those inevitable factors that every human experiences. More than not, I've rarely heard someone say "sign me up for the next dose of pain". In a world where pleasure seems to be the highest achievement of success, it feels safe to say being in pain represents failure. We as humans want to feel good all the time. In reality, it's just not possible. Unfortunately, most people die trying to achieve this pleasure principal by use of substance abuse which can lead to possible suicide due to never feeling fulfilled or lack of purpose.

The "act" of being present sometimes is that vague "I'm good" when someone asks you how you're doing. Or the smile on your face in the morning when you actually feel like crap. Or when there is an expectation of continual Joy from the person who's always producing it. Oh, wait, that's me...

There is an underlying pressure that comes with being good or being perceived as good…it produces performance. It's that notion that you are expected to be at this certain excellent level at all times. This is even expected as a child! Bananas! For an adult that is emotionally unaware, they will neglect/not take into account that the child has no vocabulary around feelings; like sadness, frustration, anger, happiness, anxiety. You know, normal things that the child possibly can't verbalize yet. The problem then becomes without proper awareness of the parent, the child begins to suppress and perform at levels of fear of failure and fear of man; human to be exact. All that to say, being "good" comes with lots of perks (attention, recognition, favor, PRESENCE) but staying "good" comes with a lot of pressure. Because when you are unable to perform you automatically doubt that you're good enough (PAIN).

I know this seems confusing how something experienced as pain can actually be good. This is a radical example but Jesus dying on the cross was good for us but it caused him much pain. There was obvious pain as blood was gushing out of his hands, feet and head. And yet he was so present to ask Father God to forgive the ones that were currently causing him pain. How Lord? If you are reading this, kiddos to you because it's safe to say you have not allowed the pain to completely take you out!

REFLECTIONS

Ways to regulate yourself...

If you're able I would recommend stretching. Start with your lower body working yourself up to the top, I also encourage playing relaxing music such as rain noises or soft instrumentals to accompany you as you stretch. As always, don't forget to breathe…deeply.

Questions:

Loss and grief aren't inclusive to losing people due to death, it can be a loss of opportunity, a physical element, even a job…etc. What has been your experience with loss, and the grief that comes with it? What do you do to help you stay present while you're feeling pain? Often when we don't want to deal with something or someone we dissociate (check out, shut down, zone out). Here are a couple of ways to help you ground yourself to help with acknowledging the pain you may presently feel.

In a seated position, place your feet on the ground, back straight at a 90-degree angle, hand placed flat on your lap, eyes open, notice 5 things in the room, listen for 3 sounds you can hear, and touch 1 thing.

Exercise

Have you ever struggled with performance? The expectancy that you have to be at a certain excellent level at all times. If so, in what ways?

What areas of your life have you accepted about yourself that you no longer need to perform in?

CHAPTER 4

SHE'LL BE COMING AROUND
THE MOUNTAIN

In 2013, my ex-girlfriend and I drove one hour and forty-five minutes outside of Redding, California, to visit Mount Shasta. It had been spoken over me more than twice while on the trip that I would climb a mountain. Upon arrival, we drove to the top, got out, and viewed. But as we sat and took in the view, I was unsatisfied and felt there was something else to see. So, we drove down the mountain. I told my ex we should go separately and meet back at this spot. So, I went left, and she went right. All I had with me was a jacket.

As I began walking on the trail, I was led into what seemed to be the woods. There were tall trees and no visible trail. I was timid about joining, but I felt like I had heard the Lord tell me he would protect me. As I entered, many things began to flutter in my mind. Let's be honest: black people don't do outdoors, but here I am, deciding to be Dora the Explorer. So now, every scary movie where a black person dies first comes to mind. But true to myself, despite the fear, I continued to walk in and appeared on a very narrow path. As I was ascending upward, I stopped and listened. It sounded like there was water under the ground. My heart began to get excited at the thought of the Lord leading me to see my first waterfall. Not a creek but a waterfall. That's just how dramatic I am to imagine. So, I kept going with the hopes of finding the beginning.

I came to a point where I was out of the woods and upon an abundance of massive white rocks. I stopped and just paused for a second. And then I heard a loud screeching sound. Fear flooded my heart immediately, and I told myself it was a baby bear. As if I knew what a baby bear sounded like, I began to play the scenario in my head. It's a lost baby bear looking for its mama, and if the mama finds it near me, she will rip me up to pieces. I became frantic; it was safe to say I froze out of my flight, fight, or freeze responses. I didn't know if I should keep going or turn back. I asked God what to do. He spoke to me and said keep going. But I felt like my feet were made of cement, and I was afraid. So, then, The Lord said he would send someone. Then, out of nowhere, a couple appeared. They were very friendly and asked if I wanted to follow them; I said yes.

We began to walk and conversate. To know me is to know I've never met a stranger. I can ask a thousand questions; having them with me felt more comfortable than being alone. As we were walking and talking, we came to a dead end. There were two arrows; one pointed left, and the other pointed right. I heard the Lord tell me to continue to the left. But just then, one of the hikers pulled out a book and said we should go right. So, I disregarded what the Lord said and left with the hikers. Shake my head, isn't that how it is sometimes? The Lord, supreme being, all-knowing heavenly father, gives you clear directions, but we still find more comfort in humans. We continued to walk, leading us to another dead end, but there was a well this time, which was where the sound of the water was coming from. The hikers felt pleased to find the well because of its significance. And to come to think of it, how often do you find a well on a mountain? But I wasn't impressed. I told them goodbye and decided to return to the dead end with the arrows and go left. I continued walking and felt like I was covering more ground alone. I looked in the distance, and I could see an open sky. I kept walking, and the view began to look familiar; it turns out I ended up in the same place where my ex and I first arrived.

I just began to laugh, and the Lord began to speak. "When you first arrived, you were already where I wanted you to be, but you became unsatisfied in fear of thinking you were missing out on more. I love your desire for more, but submitted under my guidance because your more leads you down a harder route that I did not plan but you made. You followed man, which led you to a dead end, but when you returned and listened to what I said, you ended up on top of the mountain, the view of an "endless sky." When the Lord spoke endless sky, I slowly turned my body in a 360-like motion, and the view seemed to be enhanced. Because I was so quick to leave the first time, I didn't even see that there was a whole other side of beauty. The Lord began to speak again: "This is my great love for you, which is to lead you to the abundance of who I am and show you who you are; trust in me, and there will be no more going around the mountain, but through it."

REFLECTIONS

Ways to regulate yourself...

If possible, find a trusted friend to grab food with. Being able to verbally process your thoughts and feelings with someone can make you feel heard, acknowledged and comforted. If you don't have a physical friend, talk to the Lord, he is the best listener! He knows all my tea!

Questions:

Fear is another strong emotion that is often suppressed due to its possible negative way of being expressed. When you have experienced fear, what helps you face it or get through it? Ways to help identify the root cause of fear is to speak to a mental health profession.

Have you ever felt like you were right where you needed to be but got distracted due to being curious or just disobedient? How did you get back on track?

How does the Lord speak to you? Thorough nature, by sight, audibly? Challenge yourself and ask the Lord to speak to you in a different way. Oftentimes we limit God by placing him in a box of what we've always known. God is infinite, ask him to speak to you in a new way.

CHAPTER 5

THE CHILDREN'S BREAD

It was December 26, 2019. There I was, lying on the bed. Feelings of emptiness, despair, and disappointment oppressed me. I kept replaying my sister's words she said the day before in my head. "I'm not doing another Christmas with y'all, not another holiday."

Her words pierced me, as holidays were a day for gathering with loved ones to eat and enjoy each other's company. A narrative I believed as a child about holidays was that even if we had not been in a close relationship, you must pull it together for pictures and food. With the loss of my parents, I've always felt an innate responsibility for us (my siblings) to be together no matter what. I had a constant ringing in my head of my mother's words: "Keep the family together."

My sister's displeasure came from the idol that consumed me at the time: marijuana. This drug quickly became my saving grace after my parents died. I did not want to feel the pain, so I promptly turned and sought out what I perceived as immediate pleasure. It was a ripple effect; I smoked, I ate, I watched porn, masturbated, then went to sleep. These were my coping mechanisms.

As I lay there, I drove out my sister's words by doing what she detested. I reached for marijuana edible, had my phone to the left, and my masturbating vibrator to my right, when all of a sudden, a bright presence came into my room. Audibly, it said, "LOOK, I'M ABOUT TO LEAVE YOU! I'M ABOUT TO LEAVE YOU IN WHAT YOU'RE CHOOSING! I'M ABOUT TO LEAVE YOU COMPLETELY TO YOUR SIN!"

I jumped out of bed and trembled in fear because I knew this was the voice of the Lord. I was terrified. Proverbs 9:10 states *the fear of the Lord is the beginning of wisdom, and knowledge of the Holy One is understanding.* At that moment, I realized I honestly didn't fear God or the consequences of my sin until he stated he would leave me. I couldn't comprehend what he protected me from with my human mind until he said he would leave me. Did I mention he said he was going to leave me? The one who said he would not leave nor forsake me. We all know I had abandonment issues due to my loved ones passing; now the creator said he was going to leave me. I had never denounced it before, but all I could say was, "ALL HELL, NAW."

I then heard the Lord ask for me to give him my sexual identity. According to the religious institute, *Sexual identity is an individual's sense of self as a sexual being, including gender identity, gender role, sexual orientation, and sexual concept.* Sexual identity may also refer to the language and labels people are given or used to define themselves. The development of sexual identity is critical during adolescence.

My response was what are you asking me to do? What does this have to do with you leaving me? God then began to show me how my rejection, rebellion, and bitterness toward him stemmed from those areas. But even in my fear, I felt anger boil up in me; it was like I detested the thought of giving him my sexual identity. I then said to the Lord, "How can you leave me for something you allowed, you didn't protect me when I was a child, and it led to me being raped." I didn't know at the time that this was one area I had never submitted to God due to the violation. It was an unspoken vow I hid in my heart. I felt God could have other parts of me, but not this area. He didn't protect me, so I protected me. Understanding that what he allowed to come over me became me, and now this is who I am.

In the next moment, His great love came over me gently but firmly like a warm, weighted blanket. He said, "I was there and want to show you who you truly are." I began to weep loudly in a fetal position and began repenting. For the first, I said, "Lord, I surrender to you my sexual identity, and sexual sin due to perversion. I surrender my pain and everything I've been searching for to fill my voids; tell me who I am and have your way in my life; I say yes to your will; I don't want to live without you. Can you change me? Because I've tried to change myself, but it hasn't worked". The presence of the Lord came over me again, but this time, it was cool and calmed me. I got up from the ground, the shedding of old skin, and stood to embrace the birth of my new identity.

Deliverance=salvation

Children=every person that accepts Jesus as Lord and Savior

Bread=Sustenance; support and being sustained for endurance; strength; deliverance

Deliverance is the Children's bread, and I was the child he had to deliver first!

REFLECTION

Ways to regulate yourself…

Sitting in a seat position, place your feet flat on the ground, hand flat on your lap, begin to visualize. Take a deep breath in through your nose and out through your mouth imaging your blowing out from the tip of your toes, repeat the breath and imagine your blowing out from your knees. This is called body scanning. Whatever body parts you feel comfortable with inhale and exhale, visualize yourself blowing out breath from those areas.

Questions:

Addictions are very hard to shake, especially when they stim from pain and become a sense of pleasure for escape. Have you ever struggled from any addictions? If so, what? Do you possibly know the root cause of your addiction? Ex. What happened to lead you to this addiction. Do you have people around you that can help keep you accountable to not indulge in the addiction? If so, who?

Have you ever been mad at God for something you feel he allowed? If so, what was it? Have you been able to tell him the raw feelings you have towards him? The truth is we can't hide anything from God. He sees and knows everything but he also doesn't force himself upon us, so whenever you're ready to share with him about him, he will listen!

CHAPTER 6

THE BETROTHAL

Hosea 2:19-20 "And I will betroth you (Israel) to Me forever; Yes, I will betroth you to Me in righteousness and in justice, In loving kindness and loyalty, and in compassion. I will betroth you to Me in stability and in faithfulness. Then you will know (recognize, appreciate) the Lord [and respond with loving faithfulness]".

Betrothal-enter into formal agreement to marry.

God said to me in 2020, "You have allowed so many to have access to your heart; allow me the privilege to pursue you as a lover."

It was no secret that every prior romantic relationship I participated in was dysfunctional. I had given my heart and body to those who took advantage of me. I allowed this in response to self-hate, which stemmed from my violation. My immediate response to God was, "What? How is this possible? I call you Heavenly Father, and you call me daughter…that sounds weird to think of each other in any other way."

Perversion tainted my view of pure love from the Creator, who *is* love itself. The Lord responded, "Don't box me into your definition of who you think I can be; allow me this honor." If there was anything that could reassure me that God could be more than a father, it was the film *The Shack.*

I know it's wild to believe this is my reference outside of the Bible, but I'm just being honest. The movie showed God as an African American woman and, in a later scene, God as a Native-American man. This completely blew my mind. The concept is that God can be everything we need if we allow him; God is spirit.

After this short debate in my mind, I said yes to God's request to date me. I was nervous because I did not know what to expect. I hadn't been in a relationship since 2015, and here it is, 2020. I entertained potential interests between those years but had no mutual commitment.

Something I always desired was to be pursued romantically publicly. From being in hidden relationships and secret sins, my heart desired someone's effort to claim me proudly without shame. I remember waking up the next morning after my yes to God and feeling this sweet, warm embrace greet me. Then God began saying to me, "My beloved, you are more precious and worth more than any ruby in a crown; peace is the kiss on your face, blessed is your posture, joy is your core, and love flows through your veins. Good morning!"

Listen! I was shaken. Previously, I had the old faithful, good morning beautiful text, which is the thread every guy sends out to the women he is talking to. But this completely rocked my world. I was blushing with

God, smitten by his words and embrace. I felt the purity in every word; who knew this was possible? My best friend used to tell me she had an intimate relationship with God. Which I always thought was weird. I'm like, is she having sex with God? I thought intimacy only was achieved through sex. But intimacy is a closeness, a deeper level of relationship, so how could I ever truly know God/know myself in God if I never gave him access to the inner me? Intimacy; in-to-me-see.

These supernatural encounters happened every day for months. Whether it was good morning affirmations, an in-depth study of the Songs of Solomon, forgiveness, healing, and understanding, I was delighted in my romantic relationship with God. I had never felt love like this, a healing kind of love. But only God knew that he was preparing me to be engaged two years later to my soon-to-be husband, *The Betrothal*.

REFLECTIONS

Ways to regulate yourself…

Get creative. Pull out some art supplies; crayons, colored pencil, paints, canvas or something to create on. Play some songs that help you focus your affections towards God and see what you can create.

Questions:

In what ways do you see God? As Father? Mother? Brother…Or have you never visualized him outside of Father God?

Has the Lord ever asked you to do something in preparation of what you would receive later? What was it? How did it make you feel?

Have you ever allowed the Lord to be your romantic partner? If so, share your experience. If you haven't opened your heart to this possibility, I would like you to consider this concept. Once we accept Christ as our Lord and Savior we begin to understand how the bridegroom (Christ) gave his life on the cross as a husband and wife(bride) give themselves to one another in marriage, sacrificial communion. I want to encourage you to seek God in an intimate way. Learning the depths of him, which in turn helps you learn the depths of yourself.

How deep, how high. how wide is your love for me.

-Song title: "How deep is your love"

Blessings

www.ingramcontent.com/pod-product-compliance
Lightning Source LLC
LaVergne TN
LVHW052149130726
843272LV00054B/1809